LIFELONG WRITING HABIT

THE SECRET TO WRITING EVERY DAY

CHRIS FOX

To You, The Writer.
It's time to take it to the next level.

CONTENTS

WRITE FASTER, WRITE SMARTER SERIES

5,000 Words Per Hour
Lifelong Writing Habit
Write to Market
Launch to Market
Six Figure Author
Relaunch Your Novel

INTRODUCTION

If you're holding this book, I'm guessing you'd like to become more consistent in your writing. That's the devil a lot of us wrestle with, after all. Maybe you've cranked out a book. Maybe you've cranked out several. Wherever you are in your craft, you've probably had spurts of intense creativity (yay), but have also suffered from droughts where you simply cannot force your butt into the chair to write (boo).

I have good news. This book will teach you to write consistently, every day. No exceptions. You'll learn to harness the twin powers of discipline and motivation, both of which are required if you want to crank out the volume of work necessary to make a living as a writer.

Be warned, though. This book isn't a 'One Five Minute Tip' that will give you a magic bullet to transform you into Stephen King. Writing is hard work. Our craft takes time and dedication. It takes work. Lots and lots of work. I can give you the tools, but if you're not interested in working your ass off you should close this book and save yourself a few bucks.

If you *are* willing to do the work, though, this book will change your writing life forever. I'll show you how I went from writing a few hundred words every few weeks to consistently cranking out 5,000 every day. Follow the system I teach, and you'll be doing exactly the same thing, for the rest of your life.

I could go on and on for several more pages to pad the book, but your time is valuable. Let's rock.

For Those People Who Want to Know About the Author

To my surprise, I learned with **5,000 Words Per Hour** that some people actually want to know a little bit about the person writing the books they read. That's not me. I prefer to get right into what the book can teach me without all the fluff, bragging, and all around BS from some pompous windbag author.

If you're like me this section will bore you, so skip to Chapter 1. If, on the other hand, you ARE curious, here's my story and why I'm qualified to teach you to install your lifelong writing habit.

My story began back in 2007 during the financial crisis. At the time I was an executive vice president for a mortgage bank. Don't let the fancy title fool you. It basically meant I was a sales manager for a fly-by-night lender. We were making money hand over fist, just like everyone else from 2003-2007.

One of my responsibilities was studying interest rates, so we could sell pools of mortgage loans to Wall Street, and I saw the crash coming before most people. I used the opportunity to move home to northern California, leaving Los Angeles behind. I was burnt out, exhausted, and just beginning the worst chapter of my life.

My life in Santa Rosa was dismal. I embraced my Lester Burnham moment, taking a job that paid $12 an hour for a local credit union. I didn't earn enough to make ends meet, and within a few months my savings were gone. Then the debt started to mount. My self-esteem was shot, and I quickly gained another forty pounds. Note that I was already morbidly obese, and this just made it worse.

I didn't date. Far from it. My perfect day was one

where no one noticed me, and I was able to make it home without speaking to a single person. Once there I'd obliterate the pain and shame with a healthy dose of marijuana, and then I'd play World of Warcraft until I passed out. I was the epitome of the stoned slacker, a guy in his early thirties who had exactly nothing he could point to as an accomplishment. I had no decent job prospects, no college degree, and no marketable skills. I hadn't written in over five years, despite having had a number of short stories published.

This next paragraph is exactly the kind of pompous bragging I mentioned above, but hear me out. As you read it, remember that you and I are *no different.* Anything I've done, you can do too.

I'm now the lead software engineer at a San Francisco startup. I work with people with doctorates from Harvard, Stanford, and Berkeley. Yet I, the junior college dropout, am the highest paid person at the company. I've dropped over a hundred pounds and am dating the love of my life. In the last twelve months I've also published three novels and been on some of the largest writing podcasts in the world.

I'm debt free and on track to make a quarter of a million dollars in 2015. I've become an accomplished public speaker, and have learned a whole of host of skills I never expected. Recently I even hiked the John Muir Trail, a grueling high altitude trek through the Sierras.

So where am I going with this? As I was making those changes I developed a system, and you're holding that system in your hands right now. It's short, practical, easy to understand, and full of actionable steps. If you follow that system, there's no reason you can't accomplish everything I have and more.

Trust me when I say there is *absolutely nothing special about me.* I'm where I am simply because I started installing the right habits, exactly like you're about to do.

-Chris

WHAT IS A HABIT?

Before we can begin building a habit, it's critical that you understand exactly what a habit is. Thanks to advances in neuroscience, we understand more than we ever have about habits, their creation, and how and when our brain accesses them. This study has been used by the advertising industry for decades to get you to buy everything from toothpaste to Febreze.

The good news is that you can harness the same techniques to get the same result. In essence, you'll be installing a habit in your brain just like you'd install the computer program you use to write.

Anatomy of a Habit

As mentioned above, a habit is very much like a computer program. That habit lives in a part of your brain called the basal ganglia, and it consists of three parts:

1. The Trigger
2. The Routine
3. The Reward

The Trigger is exactly what it sounds like, the event that triggers the habit. This varies from habit to habit, but every habit has one. You can confirm this by examining your own daily routine. What does your morning look like? Odds are good the alarm goes off at a specific time. That's a trigger. So is walking by Starbucks and smelling coffee.

The Routine is the meat of a habit. It's the 'what you do' part. When my alarm goes off I get out of bed, put in my contacts, and stumble off to the gym. What does your morning routine look like? Odds are good that it's the same on most days. Maybe you get up and have breakfast. Or flip on the TV. Or surf Reddit. Whatever you do, you probably do it consistently.

The Reward is the 'what you get out of it' part. In my case I get a rush of endorphins from working out, and I have the knowledge that I started off my day by getting stronger. I get to step on the scale and be happy with the number I see. If you stop by Starbucks the reward is the massive burst of sugar and caffeine.

Good Habits Versus Bad Habits

Clearly not every habit is good for us. Some lead to us gaining weight. Some waste a colossal amount of time without giving us anything to show for it. Once upon a time I devoured everything in sight, which led to me topping the scale at 303 pounds. I spent all my free time playing video games and getting high.

Each of these habits had the same three parts, and all were ultimately motivated by the reward. This revelation was huge, because as a computer programmer I found myself asking the question that prompted me to write this book. What if I could modify my habits? What if it were possible to uninstall bad ones or to install new good ones?

Flipping a Habit

I started to experiment with my morning habit. The part that was making me gain weight was the routine. The trigger (the alarm) was just fine. The reward (feeling satiated and a sense of completion) didn't need to change. What did was the specific actions I took every morning. So I tried changing the routine without modifying either the trigger or the reward.

I woke up a half hour earlier, but still with the same alarm. I went to the gym and worked my butt off. Then I stopped by Starbucks, just like I'd always done. But this time instead of a venti I got a tall. I picked a smaller pastry. I was still getting a bunch of sugar and caffeine, but I'd cut the calories I was eating in half. I'd also added a daily workout that took care of the calories I was still eating.

The new routine was difficult to maintain for the first few weeks. I'll explain more about that later when we talk about why willpower doesn't work. The takeaway here, though, is that by maintaining my new habit for three weeks I successfully flipped it. My mornings never went back to the old routine, and I started losing weight immediately.

Hopefully you're already thinking about how you can apply this principle to your own life. When you break down everything into easy to understand habits, your motivations, success (or lack of it), and desires make a lot more sense. We really are creatures of habit, and knowing that gives you immense power.

A Quick Note About Exercises

At the end of every chapter you'll find at least one exercise. You might be tempted to skip these, and keep reading. I know that's what I do. I promise myself I'll go back and do them later, but of course that rarely happens.

For that reason I've gathered all the exercises into an appendix at the end of the book. If you want to read this all in one sitting, please, please make sure you go back and do the exercises later. This book will be worthless to you if you don't put in the work to implement what it teaches.

Exercise #1- Write out your daily routine as a list of habits. Next to each of those habits put a (G) or a (B)

for good or bad. Once you've completed the list pick a habit you'd like to flip. We're going to modify that habit in future chapters, until it becomes the foundation of your daily writing. For now all you have to do is pick it!

2

PRIMING YOUR SUBCONSCIOUS

Now that you have a better idea of what a habit is, and more specifically what *your* habits are, we can begin changing them. If this sounds difficult, that's because it is. But it is also a very straightforward process that anyone can do if they're willing to put in the work.

That work begins by priming our subconscious, which is far more powerful than many of us assume.

Your Mind, the Iceberg

Picture your mind like an iceberg. Your conscious mind is the little bit of ice above the water, the 10% that ships can see. The vast expanse under the ocean, the huge 90%, is your subconscious. This part of your mind never sleeps. It is always working, and it does exactly what you program it to do.

It executes habits and notices things that you've told it are relevant. You tell it what's relevant through the simple act of deciding who you are as a person. For example, if you say that you're a bad dancer, then your mind accepts that as reality. It will subtly reinforce that belief and you may not even realize it's happening.

If, on the other hand, you decide you're a best-selling author, then your mind will subtly reinforce that. It will begin noticing the things that will help you achieve that goal, and it will keep doing so until your goal is a reality.

Your mind does this because it lacks the power to differentiate between what you think of as real, and what is actually real. Let me give you an example of how that works. Have you ever been pissed off at someone? Like really, really angry over something you thought they did? Think about how you felt physically, about the anger and pain you experienced. Then you found out that you were wrong. That person didn't do what you thought they did.

Bam. Your whole mindset shifted instantly. Maybe the new emotion was relief, or guilt. But your whole physiology changed. All based on something you *believed*, something that had no basis in reality.

Visualization

This is why almost every major athlete in the world practices visualization. They see what's going to happen before it happens, because doing so convinces their subconscious that it's already true. If you believe you're going to sell a million books this year, that you are a big league author, then your mind will do everything in its power to make that a reality.

It isn't magic and it isn't wish fulfillment. Simply believing that you're great, without backing it up with the rest of this book, won't do squat. But it is the first step, and as you continue reading you'll begin to understand why this step is so important.

Your Target Identity

If you want to write every day without fail, then you need to convince your subconscious that you're the type of author who writes every day. It needs to be a standard, an unwavering commitment to follow through every day. In this next section we're going to craft that identity, and this identity will fuel everything you do for the rest of the book.

This is the idealized version of yourself, the person you've always wanted to be. By conceiving of that person, you're taking the first step to becoming them.

Vision

This is the part I enjoy most. All writers began writing for a very specific reason. What was yours? Who did you want to become? Do you want to sell a million books? Did you want to be famous? Imagine a genie just popped out of a lamp. He'll grant your writing wish, making you into the exact author you've always wanted to be.

All you have to do is define that author. This part is very, very important. You need to see in your head exactly who you've become. How many books have you sold? What does your writing room look like? Do you live on a beach? Or in the woods? Craft the exact image of the life you'd love to lead. I don't care if that life seems impossible. You don't need to know how you're going to become this author, only that you ARE going to become them.

Remember the spiel about the subconscious a few paragraphs back? The identity you're crafting is going to reprogram your subconscious. It will have a powerful, subtle effect on your life going forward. I know this probably feels a little touchy-feely, but trust me, it works. Your mind will conceive of this new identity as reality, even though you may have a long way to go in order to make it so. Your brain will engage something called the reticular activating system (RAS) to help you.

Your RAS is the part of your brain that notices things, and you can observe it at work right now. Look around the room for something blue. If you can't find something blue, pick another color. All the objects that are that color suddenly leap to your attention. There's nothing different about them, except that you are now looking for blue objects.

You'll also see your RAS at work in daily life. Have you ever bought a certain article of clothing, or a car, and all of a sudden you started seeing it every-where? Those cars and clothes were always there, but now your RAS attaches meaning to them, so you notice them.

This principle will work exactly the same way

with your target identity. If you are a best-selling novelist, then your subconscious will start looking for people, situations, and resources that will help you achieve that goal.

Purpose

Once you've crafted your target identity and know who it is you're going to become, you have to ask yourself why. Why do you want to be a big, fancy, famous author? My answers were as follows: I want to never worry about money again. I want to tell stories that will entertain millions. I want to be able to wake up each day and do whatever I want to do.

Your purpose is important, because it lines up with the third part of every habit. The Reward. You need to understand what you're going to get out of your target identity. It needs to be compelling, because if it isn't there's no way you're going to do the massive amount of work necessary to achieve your goals.

I revisit my purpose every day. I spend at least five minutes thinking about the rewards I'll gain, about how amazing life will be when I become the person I've always dreamed of. Not only does this reinforce my target identity, but it's fun to imagine how wonderful my life will be.

The Power of Belief

I cannot overstate the power of belief. If you accept that you are meant for greatness, then you will be great. You will write every day, and you will crank out wonderful novels. Does that sound like horse crap? Consider this.

Until 1954 it was a commonly held belief that the human body could not run faster than a four minute mile. Everyone accepted that it was impossible. It simply couldn't be done. Today thousands upon thousands of people have run under a four minute mile. Many of them are *high school kids*. So what changed? On May 6th, 1954, Roger Bannister ran a mile in 3 minutes 59.4 seconds. A single person showed us it was possible. As soon as people believed it could be done, they took the first step to doing it themselves.

There are writers out there selling millions of books. There are writers publishing a novel (or more) a month. No matter how impossible your dream feels right now, you have to believe it's possible. Someone is out there doing it, and if they're doing it why can't you? Are they more talented? Probably not. Odds are good they've simply put in a whole lot of very hard work to get where they are.

You're going to do exactly the same thing, and you're going to get the same results, or better. Believe it. Be relentless in your belief, and in the actions you take to reinforce that belief. Never waver. You've got this.

The Big Questions

There is one last phase to priming your subconscious, and it's a doozy. You need to ask yourself two critical questions, and the answer to both needs to be a resounding yes. If those answers aren't yes, your subconscious will know, and we'll have a real problem installing your writing habit. So consider them carefully, and answer truthfully.

1. Is your writing goal achievable? Can you become your target identity?
2. Is it worth it?

Hopefully, you can already answer yes to #1. If

you can't, let me make something perfectly clear. ANYONE can be a great writer, provided they're willing to put in the effort. I don't care where you are in your writing journey. If you spend an hour a day for the next three years, you will be light years ahead of where you are now. Consider your target identity carefully, and BELIEVE that you will become that person. Hell, you already *are* that person. Your life just doesn't know it yet.

The second question is usually easier to give a yes to. You're going to have to work really, really hard to write every day to become the best author you can be. You're going to have to labor tirelessly in front of the keyboard, for years. Are you willing to put in that type of effort knowing that the ultimate reward is the target identity?

Exercise #2- Write a paragraph about your target identity. Hell, write three paragraphs. Make it as vivid as possible. Describe your perfect writing life, the kind you'd have if you tirelessly cranked out 5,000 words a day for the next three years.

Then write out your purpose. Why are you doing all this work?

Finally answer the two big questions. Is this achievable? Is it worth it?

Now print out a copy and put it up wherever you write. Look at it every day when you sit down to write.

Bonus: Find a picture of the house you want to own, or the beach you want to write on, or something that represents the life you're going to have when you become your target identity. Put it up next to the written description.

3

INSTALLING HABITS

Now the real work begins. Your subconscious is primed, so we're clear to work on your conscious mind. This will be much more labor-intensive, but also less touchy-feely (and thus easier to understand, at least for me).

We're going to identify the vital behaviors you have to change in order to write daily. Before we get there, it's critical you understand what willpower is, and why it doesn't work in the long term.

Why Willpower Doesn't Work

Have you ever been on a diet? Most people have, and most people not only fail at their diet, but gain an additional 2 pounds after they finish it. Yikes. I fell into that category for years, and I beat myself up constantly. I simply could not understand why I couldn't muster the willpower to eat right. I felt like a failure, but I had no idea that the deck was thoroughly stacked against me.

As it turns out willpower is a finite resource. If you like video games, imagine a little blue bar that represents willpower. It begins at full every day, provided you had enough rest. If not, your precious willpower is already partially depleted for the day. Each time you make a decision it depletes your willpower, until you have nothing remaining.

This is why advertising companies run infomercials in the middle of the night. They're after night owls, the people who had long days and haven't had a chance to recharge. That's the exact moment when those people are weakest, the most likely to make an impulse purchase.

This is also the reason why Steve Jobs wore the same shirt and jeans to work every day for years. He knew that it meant one less decision he had to make every day, which saved his precious willpower for decisions that mattered.

If you picked up this book I'm assuming you want to write more consistently. Odd are good you've tried to do this on your own, but some days you just don't write. You can't seem to muster the willpower, perhaps because you're tired. Or often because you had too many other things pressing on you, and when you'd finished dealing with them you had nothing left to give to your craft.

If that sounds like you, then I have good news. Willpower doesn't work, but habits do. Once you've installed a writing habit you'll do it every day without thinking. If you miss a day you'll have this nagging feeling that something didn't get done, and you'll get right back at it the next day.

I know this, because I've installed a writing habit in my own life. I haven't missed a day for over a year, and I've only missed a handful in the last two years.

Vital Behaviors

So if willpower isn't the answer, then what is? Vital behaviors. These are the behaviors that are most critical to your success, the cornerstone habits that will ripple through your entire life.

When I was losing weight the single most vital behavior was stepping on the scale every day. The second was recording every last morsel of food that I ate. The combination of the two forced me to be accountable to myself. I knew that if I reached for that second piece of pizza I'd have to face the scale the following morning. I'd have to log it in My Fitness Pal and see that I'd overshot my calories for the day.

The same principle works for writing. You need to be accountable, and that means tracking your output. You need to log every day that you write, including how many words you cranked out. Doing so won't just encourage you to get your butt in the chair every day, it will also inspire you to do better than the day before. If you hit 1,000 words, your brain will push you to do 1,200.

What this means is that, in the short term, you don't need to worry about *what* you write. You don't need to worry about finishing projects (yet). All you need to do is make sure you sit in the same chair, ideally in the same place, every day. If you train your brain to write at 6 am, seven days a week, then the hardest work is done.

Tend to that one vital behavior and the rest will fall into line almost of their own accord. Your subconscious will begin nudging you, gradually correcting the rest of your habits. You'll write faster, and you'll become more productive the longer you stick to the vital behavior of sitting in the chair every day and tracking your output.

Three Weeks to Success

This does mean that you need at least a little bit of discipline to get the ball rolling. A habit takes roughly 21 days to fully install, but each day you repeat the habit you'll gain more momentum. Later in the book we'll discuss some tools that will help make the first three weeks easier, but for now take heart.

If you can convince yourself to write *tomorrow*, then you're one step closer to three weeks. Every day you write puts you one step closer, and once you cross that finish line your habit will be installed. Writing will be a must, a daily need that is as automatic as buying a cup of coffee or going to the gym.

Exercise #3- Decide how you are going to track your writing habit. Maybe you need a physical calendar, where you jot the words down on the date each time you write. Maybe you use a spreadsheet. Maybe you download the 5000 Words Per Hour app I wrote to track writing sprints (if you have an iPhone or iPad).

The method you choose is completely up to you, but the critical factor here is that you MUST track your daily writing. You must log the date, and the number of words you wrote. I know that sounds small, but this will have a POWERFUL effect on your writing.

4

YOUR FINGER PAINTING SUCKS

T his was probably my favorite chapter to write, both because of the title and the meaning behind it. One of the primary reasons people quit writing is the finger painting syndrome. If you want to write daily you need to know what it is, and how to avoid the trap it presents. Finger painting syndrome is baked into American life, and as I understand it from foreign friends it's present elsewhere too. So what is it?

When we were children, we were praised for everything. If a five year old paints a crappy finger painting we pat them on the head, tell them how amazing they are, and then put it on the refrigerator. On the surface, this makes a lot of sense. If you tell a five year old that their finger painting sucks, they'll start bawling and most likely never paint again.

Here's where the problem arises. At some point the coddling needs to stop, or we learn that our first effort is always amazing, even when it isn't. By the time we graduate from high school we've been convinced that we're going to be rock gods and movie stars, authors and presidents. Yet what we haven't learned is that achieving such goals takes an immense amount of work. We expect it to come easily, because we've always been praised for the tiniest bit of effort.

This is especially true for gifted kids. I never learned to study in school, and barely showed up for class. I still got As, because the classes were easy for me, and I came out of school with a major chip on my shoulder. Then I met the real world. No one gave a shit that I was a special snowflake, especially where my writing was concerned.

I believed that my first novel would be amazing, and that publishers would line up to give me millions. Yet when I finished that first book I couldn't even get friends to read it, because it was terrible. My finger painting sucked. So I quit writing for five years, convinced that I'd never be a real writer.

Anyone Can Write

I gave in to the great lie that writers are born, not made. That's a huge pile of horse shit. Anyone can write, as long as they put in the time and effort to learn their craft.

In high school everyone *knew* I was going to be a writer. I was praised constantly for essays and short stories. Yet as I mentioned above as soon as it became difficult I quit. I have a friend who didn't. In high school we called his writing Saul-speak, because it was nearly impossible to read. Most words were misspelled. Those that weren't were often the wrong word (*two* instead of *too*).

He was terrible, yet he wanted to be a novelist. I quit. He didn't. A decade later he had two novels published and I had none. Saul worked on his craft tirelessly, deliberately practicing skills every day. That dedication made him a great writer, despite the fact that in high school everyone would have told you what he wanted to accomplish was impossible.

So how is this relevant to you? Because if you're going to write you need to go in with eyes wide open, and you need to learn to embrace criticism.

Criticism Is Your Best Friend

I quit writing twice more in my adult life, both times after someone told me how terrible a piece of writing was. I was so proud of my finger paintings, but they just weren't good enough. I proudly showed them to my parents (readers), and they were slapped down as the flawed crap they were. I couldn't handle it, so rather than listen to what people were telling me I gave up.

Fast forward to today. I just sent out the manuscript for *Vampires Don't Sparkle* to my beta readers. It's a team of nearly a hundred people, and as of this writing I've heard back from about 25. Almost all of them said the same thing. 'Wow, this is great.'

That feedback doesn't help me. It fluffs my ego a little, but I know there are big problems with the manuscript. I just need help identifying them. Only three beta readers have had useful criticism, and those people are my heroes. They cheerfully tell me what sucks about the book, which enables me both to fix this novel and to learn what not to do in the future.

We only grow by making mistakes, and the actual growth occurs when you learn from those mistakes. If you get upset at yourself or quit at the first sign of criticism you'll never make it as a writer. You sure as hell won't write every day.

So grow a thick skin. Convince yourself that you're in first grade. You'll graduate from high school someday, but until then every manuscript is a paper you're turning in to be graded. Each time someone points out a flaw, consider it a gift. Learn from it, and make the next thing you write better.

If you can cultivate this mindset, you're one step closer to daily writing, because bad reviews, critical beta reader feedback, and even haters and trolls simply won't faze you.

You're in this for the long haul, and in five years you'll be an immeasurably better writer. Don't get hung up on where you are now.

Exercise #4- Search your hard drive, email, or file cabinet for the oldest piece of your writing you can find. Go back and read it with a critical eye. What have you learned since then? How has your writing improved? Look at all the progress you've made since then. Imagine how much better you'll be in a year if you practice daily.

5

GETTING ORGANIZED

I mentioned in previous chapters that tracking your writing habit is key. So key that it is the *single most vital behavior* to the creation and maintenance of your writing habit. If you take nothing else away from this book, the need to track daily writing output should be it. In this chapter we're going to take that a step further. Tracking is key, but organization and a plan will amplify the power of your tracking.

Some of what you'll learn in this chapter may not feel applicable to your writing habit, but trust me when I say it is very much worth knowing. Writing isn't an isolated part of your life, and making changes in other areas will very much improve your writing too.

Decluttering Your Mind

In 2010 I read a life-changing book called *Getting Things Done*. The book presented a simple system for organizing your life, one that I've used ever since. What made the system so attractive to me wasn't the specifics. It was the immediate benefits I saw.

Prior to adopting this system I spent every day in a constant state of stress. I was always worrying about a dozen tasks I had to do, from returning phone calls to running errands. I'm a pretty smart guy, but things fell through the cracks. I missed appointments, forgot birthdays, and had to live with the guilt of knowing I was unreliable.

The very first week I implemented the GTD system that all changed. Instead of worrying about things, I knew that every task I had to take care of had been deposited into a trusted system. I didn't need to worry about them, because I knew that my system would take care of that for me.

This simple act decluttered my mind, and it did a lot more than simply reduce my stress. It made me a more creative writer, because once you remove all the daily burdens filling your mind you create room for wonderful stories.

I highly recommend reading *Getting Things Done*, but the rest of this chapter will present a simplified system that will give you many of the same benefits.

Pick a Project Management Tool

If you already have a tool you like to use, wonderful! You're already ahead of most people. If not, I'll go through a few of the great ones. Each is available for Android or iPhone, and many are also available on PC or Mac.

All these tools have something in common. They allow you to create both tasks and projects, a project simply being something that will take more than one task to complete. For example:

Task- Buy Milk

Project- Finish Vampires Don't Sparkle
    Send beta draft to Alida for editing
    Integrate feedback
    Write next draft
    Send draft to Tammi for line editing

The goal is to have a tool where you put *everything*. Every birthday, every errand, every project, even your bucket list items. Get everything you should do, everything you want to do, and everything you need to do out of your head and into a system you'll check every day.

Omnifocus- This is by far my favorite tool, and one I've used for years. It was designed to work with *Getting Things Done*, so if you read that book this software is perfect. It tracks projects, calendar items, and most importantly context. Contexts are basically tags, so, for example, you can group all of your errands in one place. Then, when you're out of the house running an errand you can quickly look to see if there are one or two more you can easily do.

The software is available on iPhone, iPad, and Mac and it rocks. The only downside is that it's expensive. If you have the money to spend this app is wonderful. If not, some of the ones below will work just as well.

Things- This was the first app that I used to get organized. It's not terribly expensive, but is only available for Mac and iOS. It tracks projects, and has areas which are similar to the contexts used in Omnifocus.

There are about eight billion tools I haven't listed. If you don't want to use one of the above, use your smartphone to browse the app store for 'project management' and find one you think will work. Feel free to experiment with several until you find one you like. It will be worth the effort. If you find and use an app like this daily, you will all but guarantee a successful daily writing habit.

You'll also simplify your life in general, and I can't even begin to stress how amazing this change will be. Living every day without constant worry and stress is the single largest quality of life change you can make!

Organize Your Email

One of the other major life changes GTD showed me was organizing my inbox. Prior to the book I had six or seven thousand emails going back at least five years. There was no end to my inbox, just emails I'd read and emails I hadn't. I regularly forgot to reply to emails, because if I received a bunch of new ones the old ones quickly fell off the page.

If I had time I might scroll down and check them, but if life was hectic weeks could go by before I scrolled down. I can't count the number of emails that fell through the cracks, which resulted in me dropping the ball all over the place.

GTD presents a simple system to gain control over your inbox. The rule is simple. You process your email by going through every email in your inbox. Each email is touched only once, and you do one of the following:

1. Reply to it.
2. File it into an actionable folder you'll check later that day (and will check every day).
3. Add it to a reference folder if it has info you'll need later.
4. Add it to an incubate folder if it's something you might not need to see for a month or two (like a concert you might attend in several months).

5. Delegate it (forward it to someone else to deal with).

By implementing this simple system I got my inbox down to 0, and I never have more than ten emails in there. I recently left for three weeks to hike the John Muir Trail, and came back to almost 1,500 emails. Using the system above, I cranked through them all in two hours, and as it turned out there were only about 40 that needed an actual response.

The feeling of having an empty inbox every day is incredibly empowering. You know you're handling the things that need to be handled, and it makes you feel on top of the world. This increases your mental freedom, which gives you more time to focus on the things that really matter in life. Like the section above, I cannot stress how much this change will increase your quality of life.

Organize Your Writing

Now for the part you've been waiting for, organizing your writing. I want to stress that the following is my system, but you need to create a system that works for you. If mine is too complex, or too simple, then change it to suit your needs.

I begin by creating a project for every writing idea I have. Every short story, blog post, novel, non-fiction book, and speech gets its own project. You can create these projects in the software you chose above, or if you'd prefer you can create an actual file folder for each. How you manage them is up to you, but the important thing is that you create a place-holder for every last story.

Most of us have a huge list of projects, one that's always growing. That's totally okay. Some of your projects will eventually go into the garbage. Others may gather virtual dust for years before being touched. The trick is to get them out of your head and into your tracking system. Doing this allows you to focus on one idea, instead of flittering about between dozens.

Once you've created your entire list of projects, pick the two or three you're most excited about working on. I typically select a blog post, a novel, and a non-fiction book. These go in an 'Active' folder at the top of my project list in Omnifocus. These are the projects I check every day.

I sort the rest of them by type. Then when I'm ready for a new project of the appropriate type it's as easy as selecting one of the appropriate type. This may not sound like it's that important, but trust me, it will become clear in the next chapter why this is such a useful habit to adopt.

Spring Cleaning

Once a month I go through my project lists and evaluate each. Some are moved up in priority, a few are abandoned, and the rest generally get a few notes. This process is important, because if you keep adding to your list without ever taking away, you'll eventually develop a mental aversion to your system.

Keeping your system fresh prevents this, which gives you that mental freedom I mentioned earlier.

Exercise #5- This one is a biggie. Develop your system. Either choose an app, or create a pen and paper system where you can track your writing projects. Then write down every project you can think of until every last one is out of your head and in the system.

Bonus 1- Clear your inbox using the methodology above. Practice keeping it clean for a week. The results will probably surprise you.

Bonus 2- Put *all* your projects into your system, not just the writing ones. This will have a massive impact on your overall productivity and happiness, plus you'll be more attractive.

6

PROPINQUITY

Propinquity is a funny word most people haven't heard of, yet every one of us is aware of the effects. The definition is 'the study of how time and distance affect human behavior', but that doesn't really tell you squat, does it?

Let me give you an example that will make it clear exactly what propinquity means. Let's say you're driving home from work, and you pass by a fast food restaurant. The instant you see the sign you start craving your favorite cheeseburger. You glance at the drive through and realize there's not a single car in line. Before you're even consciously aware of it you're turning into the driveway and ordering your tasty dinner.

Now let's modify the scenario above. You glance

at the drive through and you see fifteen cars waiting. It's going to take you 20 or 30 minutes to get your burger. What do you do? You keep driving. That's propinquity at work. People are inherently lazy, meaning we'll take the path of least resistance. You can see this just by looking at your own behavior in every day scenarios.

In essence, propinquity studies how small barriers will influence your behavior. This is critical to your success as an author, and you can harness propinquity to set you up for massive success. You can use this process to put your writing habit on rails, all but guaranteeing that you hit daily goals. Below we'll discuss some of the ways you can use propinquity, and as you read some of my suggestions see if you can come up with your own. Once you understand this principle you'll view the world around you in an entirely different light.

Removing Barriers From Good Behaviors

The first use for propinquity is removing all the little barriers that will keep you from writing. The more of these exist, the less likely you are to write. Many of them are simple, and some so tiny you may doubt that they'll keep you from writing. But they will. So here are a few ways you can remove barriers:

1. Make sure your word processor is open to the project you want to work on the night before.
2. Close down the applications that might distract you from writing.
3. Use the bathroom and get a beverage before you sit down, so you don't have an excuse to stop writing and go do that.
4. Put your phone on silent, or better yet turn it off for the duration of your writing.

Erecting Barriers Around Bad Behaviors

In the same way you want to remove barriers that will stop you from writing, you also want to erect barriers that will prevent you from doing things other than writing. Here are some examples:

1. Set an alarm, alert, or reminder (or all three) that will go off every day at the time you've selected to write.

2. Add a daily 'to do' item you can check off each day once you've completed your writing. It's very satisfying, trust me.

3. Tell your friends and family that you're writing every day. This will encourage you to follow through, or you'll have to admit to them that you aren't hitting your goals.

4. Set up an app like Freedom to block the internet during the time you're supposed to be writing.

5. Better yet, take your laptop somewhere where there is no internet, and no other distractions. Practice writing there.

Exercise #6- Make a list of your biggest distractions, the things that most often prevent you from writing. Maybe that's binge-watching Scrubs on Netflix. Maybe it's being constantly interrupted by loved ones in need of help. Whatever they are, see if you can brainstorm some ways to erect barriers around the things that are preventing you from writing.

Bonus: Do the same thing for the good behaviors. Make a list of things that will simplify your writing, so that all you have to do is sit down at your computer and GO.

7

MORNINGS ARE YOUR FRIEND

What time do you get up in the morning? If you're anything like I used to be the answer is 'as early as I have to get to work or take care of the kids, but no earlier'. I used to hate mornings, and would sleep in as late as possible. I often stayed up past midnight, usually mindlessly surfing the web, or maybe watching a TV show.

Back in 2010 I made the fateful decision to get up a little earlier. At the time, I needed to be at work at 8 am and had been getting up at 7. I decided to start getting up at 6:15 so I could go to the gym. That decision changed my life forever. I found that I generally still went to bed around the same time, but that I had a jump start on the day. I spent 45 minutes working out and thinking, and by the time I got to work I was in a totally different place than I'd been when waking up at 7.

This process intrigued me, so I started getting up earlier and earlier. First I pushed the alarm to 6. Then 5:30. Then 5:15. Finally I pushed it back to 5am, where it's been for the last four solid years. During that time I've published several novels, went from making $35,000 a year in collections to being a self-taught iOS developer making well into the six figures, lost over a hundred pounds, learned a host of interesting skills from neuroscience to anthropology, and have mastered public speaking. Nearly all of these only became possible because I was getting up early, especially when combined with getting organized.

The Benefits of Waking Up Early

Now let's get into the hard scientific benefits of waking up early. We've all heard the saying 'early to bed, early to rise makes a man healthy, wealthy and wise'. This saying exists for a reason, and it turns out that neuroscience backs it up. During the night your body is healing. Muscle is rebuilding. Damage is repaired.

For your brain, something else interesting happens. Most conscious thought happens in your pre-frontal cortex, the area right behind your forehead. During the day it swells, and as this happens you develop something called pre-frontal dysfunction. In English, you get cranky because you're tired. Anything creative becomes more difficult, your temper gets shorter, and you notice less of your surroundings.

If you get a good night's sleep, this process is reversed. The swelling goes down and the neurological pathways are repaired. You wake up fresh, with a full bar of willpower. This is the absolute perfect time to write, and it's the reason I get up at 5am. I go to the gym, which elevates my heart rate and gives me time to think. By the time I get home at 6, I'm wide awake and brimming with ideas. When I sit down to write most of the world is still asleep. All the distractions and burdens of the day haven't happened yet, and I can crank out 5,000 words before everyone else is even awake.

This is huge for several reasons. For starters, it means that my writing gets done before anything else. Brian Tracy has a great book called *Eat That Frog*, and the gist is simple. Do the most important, hardest thing that you have to each day. Do it first, and then you know that it got done. I begin the day by working on my body, then I work on my mind by writing. After that I expand it further by listening to podcasts, audiobooks, and interviews.

By the time I arrive at the office around 8:15 am I've done more than most people will all day. I get to walk around knowing that my big goals were accomplished, and it feels amazing. All because I'm willing to get up a bit earlier than most other people. Growing up, I hated mornings. Now I'm a 'morning person'. I put that in quotes, because like so many things in our life it's just a self-created label. Most of us make assumptions about who we are as people, as if we're powerless to change. That's total BS. I don't care if you've never gotten up early before. Not only can you do it, but you can learn to love it.

The Cost of Waking Up Early

Yep, there's a cost to waking up at 5 am every morning. Fortunately, it's very slight. I'm almost always in bed by 9 pm. Staying up until 11 requires a massive dose of caffeine, and I definitely pay a price the next morning. If you make the commitment to waking up early, it will most likely mean going to bed earlier as well. This can take a toll on your social life, but trust me when I say it's worth it. If you're like most writers you're probably an introvert anyway, and whether you are or not you need to ask yourself if you're really serious about this writing thing. You want to write every day and crank out multiple novels a year? Then you're going to need to make some changes, and this is one that can carry you the furthest.

The cost is slight, especially when you consider how your brain works. You are freshest in the morning, so why not capitalize on your best hours? If you wait to write until the end of a long day you might do it. Or you might spend the evening watching Game of Thrones. If you wake up and write, you know it got done. You also know you did your best writing. If you wait until you're exhausted to sit down and write, I promise you that you aren't doing your best work.

I know, because I get to see this every day. I crank out my first three thousand words before I go to work. On the bus ride home I make myself crank out two thousand more. Not only are those words harder to write, but I can see the difference in quality. My best work happens when I'm fresh, and neuroscience makes it very clear why that is.

Exercise #7- Set your alarm 15 minutes earlier than normal. Before you go to bed have your computer primed and ready. Use propinquity to make sure all you have to do is sit down and write. When you wake up write for 10 minutes. See how it feels. You probably won't be very fast at first, but that's okay. If you repeat this every day you'll improve rapidly. If you like the process you can increase the time you write.

Bonus: Download my 5,000 Words Per Hour App, or use a timer to conduct a writing sprint. If you aren't familiar with the process, feel free to check out *5,000 Words Per Hour* the book, which explains how writing sprints work and how you can maximize your writing time. Reading 5KWPH isn't necessary to developing a writing habit, but it will make you far more productive, which is especially handy for those of us with busy lives.

8

GOAL SETTING

There's just one final step before you have to get your butt in the chair and start the actual daily writing. That's goal setting. This is an amazingly useful tool for every part of your life, but will be immensely useful here. I want you to think of it as the bridge between your target identity and the person you are now. This is the vehicle that will get you from here to there.

Before we get into the nitty gritty, I want to recount a Harvard University study that you might find interesting. In 1979 the Harvard MBA class was given a survey about their goals. 84% had none. 13% had them, but didn't write them down. In 1989 the same class was surveyed again.

The remaining 3%, those that had clear, written

goals, made more than the other 97% *combined*. The single difference between them and the rest of their peers was writing down their goals. Wow. Crazy, right?

Goals are powerful, powerful stuff. Remember all that talk about priming your subconscious? Writing down a goal makes it real to your brain. Thousands of successful people, myself included, can attest to this fact. Jim Carrey carried a check in his wallet that he'd written to himself. It was in the amount of $10,000,000 'for acting services rendered'. He even dated the check, and signed a deal for ten million dollars just two months before the check's date.

I'm not trying to sell you on abundance mindset. This isn't *The Secret*, and I'm not telling you that the universe will provide whatever you need if you simply believe it will. What I'm saying is that your brain is the most powerful computer ever created, and that it will manifest the reality you want it to. It will work tirelessly to achieve almost anything, but for it to do that you need to tell it what you want it to achieve.

To that end we're going to discuss two general types of goals, both of which will help you create and sustain your lifelong writing habit.

Short Term Goals

We'll begin with short term goals, the things you want to accomplish every day. These should include how many words you want to write each day (WPD if you've read 5,000 Words per Hour), how long your writing sessions should be, and how often you intend to write.

Many of my author friends write five days a week. They give themselves the weekends off, which seems to work for them. I write seven days a week, because I love what I do. For me it isn't work, it's a fun way to pay rent. So I write every day, including holidays. That works for me. You have to set up a habit that will work for you.

Your habit should also include a time you plan to write. Not just 'I'll write for a half hour each day', but 'I'll get up at 6 am and write for 30 minutes'. Be as specific as possible, because this is the kind of specificity that your subconscious latches on to. If you tell it exactly what you intend to do, then your brain will help you do it.

Remember the chapter on propinquity? Write your goal down in your project management system.

If you intend to get up every weekday at 6, then create a reminder that wakes your butt up at 6 am. Make it something you can check off, so you're tracking your goal each and every day.

Long Term Goals

These are the types of goals most of us are much more familiar with. Where do you want to be in six months? How many words do you want to have written? Will you have completed a novel? More than one? These goals need to match your short term, meaning that if you want to write 200,000 words in the next six months you need to make sure your daily writing goal will lead to that.

This will have a powerful effect, and not just on your subconscious. Remember the section on the power of belief? If you know you need to write 2,000 words a day for the next two months to finish the draft of your novel, then you can SEE that it's possible. You understand exactly what you need to do to accomplish your goal, and that makes it far, far more likely that you will.

Big, nebulous things scare us. The human brain

has a need to recognize and categorize, and by giving it specific goals to latch on to you ensure that's exactly what will happen.

Finishing What You Start

Earlier I mentioned that, at least in the beginning, it doesn't matter *what* you write. That's definitely true, but only in the beginning. One of your longterm goals should be to finish projects that you begin. If you don't do this, then you risk giving up your habit. It's very easy to rationalize abandoning your daily habit if you can say to yourself that you'll never finish anything anyway. You need to know that it's going to take you three months to finish this book, and then you need to do the daily work necessary to do exactly that.

If you do, if you are able to finish a project, you'll gain the power of momentum. Your morale will go up, and you'll learn to love writing because you'll know that you can be successful at it. The reason so many new writers struggle to crank out their daily words is because they know they suck. They believe they'll never finish, because they've never finished before. Break the cycle by finishing projects. Start with smaller projects if you need to. Finish a blog post. Or a short story. Whatever it is, teach yourself that you can complete projects, and you'll approach your daily writing with much more enthusiasm than ever before.

More importantly, you'll improve, because you'll experience every part of storytelling. Completing projects exposes you to everything from pacing to character arcs to themes. The more often you do it, the better you get.

Chunking

Chunking is the act of making many things into one, which is easier for your brain to comprehend. It's useful, because that kind of symbolic representation keeps you from freaking out.

When you are confronted by a massive project, your mind often recoils in horror. The idea of writing six novels in a year, or even writing your first novel if you're new at this, causes complete system shut down. You simply cannot wrap your brain around what's involved, so you don't. You give up before you really begin.

I'll give you an example that most of us have been through, so you can see this at work. Remember the first time you drove a car? You had to track the brake, the gas, maybe a clutch, the gearshift, the blinker, the side view mirrors, the rear view mirror, traffic signs, other cars, etc, etc. It was incredibly daunting for me. Quite frankly, I was terrified and as a result I didn't learn to drive until I was 19.

Today, when I get in the car, I don't consciously think about any of those things. Now all of that has been chunked down to one thing. Driving. I'm willing to bet the same is probably true for you. You just *drive* now, right? By installing your writing habit, you're doing the same thing with writing.

Right now you're thinking about plotting, characters, deadlines, and a million other things. Let that go. You're writing, just that one thing. When you approach it that way, everything becomes a lot simpler and your mind has a much easier timer tackling large projects.

Just make sure you *write* every day. Maybe today that's plotting. Maybe tomorrow that will be editing. Regardless of the individual daily task, it's all writing. And you're a writer, so you've got this.

The Building Block Approach

Back in the stone age, when the word for fire was *guuuuuhhhhh,* I took my first semester of college at Santa Rosa Junior College. One of the very first courses I enrolled in was Introduction to Computer Programming, which changed my life forever. Our textbook taught us to implement something it called the building block approach. In a nutshell, you reduce a massive problem into as many smaller problems as possible. Then you solve the smaller problems, and before long you realize you've solved the really big problem that was so daunting in the beginning.

Our brains have a much easier time tackling large projects when we break them down into manageable pieces. This is why the building block approach is perfect for writing books, which are a huge undertaking.

When I decide to write a new novel, I break it down into the first draft, which is further broken down into act 1, act 2, and act 3. Then I break down each act into chapters. All this happens before I've written a word of fiction, which allows me to see the whole book before I get started.

This makes it much easier to tackle, because I know that this week I'm writing chapters 1-10 in act one. Next week I'll do 11-20, and so on. I can predict when I'll have the first draft done, and then I'll do the same building block model to do the first edit (which I'll cover more in Write Faster, Write Smarter book 3).

No matter how large a problem is, if you break it down then you can solve it.

Exercise #8- Write out your short term goals for your daily habit. When will you start? How long will you write? How many words are you aiming for each day? Be as specific as possible. Then write out your long term goals, ideally for the next 12 months. Where do you want to be in a year? How many books will you write? How long will each take using your short term goals?

Bonus: Create reminders both for your short term and long term goals. Your calendar or smartphone should notify you when a goal comes due. Each day it will ping you to let you know you should be writing, and it should also notify you when it expects a project to be completed (I'll have *Vampires Don't Sparkle* re-written and submitted to Tammi by September 28th. Bam, I get a reminder on September 28th checking to make sure I did that).

9

THE POWER OF YOUR PEERS

One of the most common obstacles to a writing habit is hiding right in front of you. It's your mom. Your spouse. Your friends. Your co-workers. We are very much the product of our environment. Who you choose to associate with is who you become.

I can't speak for you, but several years back I was surrounded by some very negative people. When I'd say something outrageous like 'I'm going to teach myself to develop iPhone apps and then go out and get an amazing six figure job' those people were quick to list all the reasons I'd fail. They weren't doing it because they were jealous (though a few were). They were doing it out of love. They didn't want me to get my hopes up, because they worried what would happen when (not if) I failed.

They do this because most of these people have stopped dreaming. They don't share your vision for an amazing future. Life has ground them down to be 'practical'. To get a day job and do what's expected of them. In short, *people who can't see it for themselves can't see it in you*. This mindset is both incredibly damaging and incredibly dangerous, and by now you know the reasons why.

There's a whole other breed of negative people you need to watch out for. These are the grumps, the people who always complain, about everything. They're quick to tell you all the things that are wrong with the world. They're never happy, and are the eternal pessimists. In short, it's the Eeyore crowd. They suck the joy out of the room whenever they enter it, and that's incredibly dangerous to anyone trying to accomplish great things. You don't want to be surrounded by Eeyores. You want to be surrounded by Tiggers.

It's a sad fact that we will adopt the attitudes of the people we associate with. If your average social gathering is four people getting together to gripe about their crappy jobs, mounting bills, and various aches, then you're going to start doing the same thing. You have to cut those types of people out of your life. Otherwise, you'll allow this kind of negativity to poison your thinking, and you'll give up. You'll give in to the big lie, that it's impossible to accomplish all the crazy dreams rattling around in your head. So what do you do if you're surrounded by this kind of negativity?

Protect Your Dream

Do not ever let someone tell you that you can't achieve your dreams. If you want to become the target identity you created, then you need to believe it's possible. Listening to your friends and family tell you that it isn't undermines everything you're trying to accomplish.

This can mean that you have to make some very difficult decisions. In my case it meant ruthlessly culling my circle of friends. I stopped spending time with the most negative people, because I started to see the toll it was taking on my mindset. They were toxic, and time with them was damaging my desire. So I stopped spending time with them.

I realize that sounds harsh, but you need to ask yourself the big questions again. Is your dream possible, and *are you willing to do the work to achieve it*? It can mean making some hard choices.

Now don't get me wrong. I'm not suggesting you divorce your spouse or stop talking to your mother. I don't want you to dump all your friends and become a hermit. What I do want you to do is take a hard look at who you're spending time with, and the type of message they're sending.

If talking to your spouse about your writing leads to them telling you to give up, then stop talking to them about it. The same holds true for your mom, dad, boss, or anyone else. If you're not getting the kind of support you need from them, then stop looking for it. If there are people who are negative about your dreams even after you stop talking about them, then you need to disassociate yourself from them. Trust me, it will change your life.

Few decisions have impacted my quality of life as much as dumping toxic relationships.

Find a New Peer Group

Remember, you're the sum of your peer group. If you associate with people who have no ambition and spend all their time getting high and playing video games, then that's what you're going to become. This happens because we are a tribal species. Your standards will rise or fall to match the people you associate with. We've all heard of peer pressure, and it's a real thing. If you're doing great in every area of your life, then your friends who aren't will feel threatened. They'll begin to sabotage your success, even if only subconsciously.

You combat this by finding a new peer group. In 2010 my peer group was a couchful of stoned slackers, and I was nothing but an average member of that group. One of the keys to changing my life was finding people with as much or more ambition than I had. The kind of people who wanted to achieve big things. When I went out and met them, my standards went up instantly. I wanted more for myself so that I could fit in with my new chosen peer group.

You can do the exact same thing. Maybe you need to join a Toastmasters public speaking club. Not only will you learn about public speaking, and about leadership, but you'll also be surrounded by a room full of people who also want to improve their lives. That kind of enthusiasm and ambition is contagious, and will help propel you to the next level.

If you're an introvert and don't like getting together in person, then find an online group. There are dozens of writing forums like the Writer's

Cafe over at Kboards. There are private Facebook groups. There are even Meetups you can attend. Where you go doesn't matter, as long as you're meeting like-minded people who share your goals. You'll be amazed how empowering it is to be surrounded by other authors who face the same struggles you do.

Some of them will be ahead of you, some of them behind. You'll grow, both from learning and from teaching. That's exactly the kind of growth that will propel you toward your target identity, and I highly recommend you harness a peer group to help you do it.

Find a Mentor

If you want to be successful in any area of your life, then find someone who already has the success you're after. Ask them how they did it, and listen very careful to the answer. Most people are more than happy to help, especially if you're polite and grateful. When I first started publishing, I approached my favorite author and started asking him questions. Not only did he respond, but he was all too happy to help me. The answers helped shape the writer I became. I started approaching other authors, and learning from them as well.

I've had several mentors over the last three years, and every last one has helped me grow immensely as a writer. You need to do the same thing. Who is your favorite author? Can you send them an email? Or at least start hanging out on forums or social media where you can associate with them? It may sound impossible, but think about it from their perspective. A few years ago they were in the same boat you are, trying to make it. They can understand your struggle better than anyone, and have almost certainly gotten over all the hurdles you're about to face.

A lot of those people still have impostor syndrome, just like you. They're all too happy to help, because they realize they're not so different from up and coming writers.

Exercise #9- Write down the top five supporters in your life. These are the people who empower and support you, and also the people you should be spending more time with. If you don't have five, or don't have any, that's okay. Now write down the top five negative people in your life. These are the people who are always complaining, the people who tell you that 'it can't be done'. Almost all of us have at least one, so write down up to five.

Now take a hard look at both lists. Brainstorm ways to spend more time with the positive column. If the positive column is empty, I want you to email me at chris@chrisfoxwrites.com. I'd be proud to be the first person you add to that column, and I'm happy to connect you with like-minded people.

On the negative list, you need to make a decision about each person. Is this someone you should be associating with? Or are they the type of psychic vampire who will suck away your positive energy? If they're the latter, is there any reason to keep them in your life? If you have to (in the case of family), how can you minimize the impact they have on your daily life?

Bonus: Email your favorite author and ask them to be your mentor.

10

SELF-IMPROVEMENT

The key to long term success is lifelong improvement. Either you're getting better, or you're getting worse. Stagnation is the enemy, because it leads to apathy. Fortunately, you're already in the 1%, the people who commit to continuous growth. I know that, because not only did you buy this book, but you've read to this point. The vast majority of people never even consider picking up a self-help book. Most of those who do never even crack the cover, much less do the exercises or implement what it teaches. (You are doing the exercises, right?)

If you want to achieve the target identity you created, then you have to *commit* to lifelong improvement. You have to decide, right now, that you're willing to do the work. Willing to do whatever it takes to achieve your dream. If you do that, then I have great news. The tools are already out there. Everything you need to become an ass-kicking, novel-writing machine is at your fingertips.

This book is just the beginning, a first step to unlocking your vast untapped potential.

Learn to Love Learning

I'm borrowing a concept from Tony Robbins, a principle that continues to change my life to this day. He suggested turning your vehicle into a mobile university. Instead of listening to music and daydreaming, start listening to audiobooks. What skills do you want to learn? Are there other writing books you want to pick up? Are you looking for motivation? There are dozens of great audiobooks to choose from, and I've included a partial list here:

- *Getting Things Done* by David Allen
- *Eat that Frog* by Brian Tracy
- *The Success Principles* by Jack Canfield
- *The Power of Habit* by Charles Duhigg

In addition to audiobooks there are some

amazing podcasts you can check out. Many are geared toward writers, some are geared at anyone wanting to be successful. Here's a list of my favorites, all of which are available on iTunes or Stitcher:

- Rocking Self-Publishing
- The Author Biz
- Self Publishing Podcast
- Fantasy & Science Fiction Marketing Podcast
- The Sell More Books Show
- The Creative Penn
- Smart Passive Income
- The Eventual Millionaire

One of the ways you can improve your life is by filling yourself with great ideas. The podcasts and books listed above will help you do it, and you can do it without putting in any extra time. Just start listening on the bus, or in the car, or on the tread-mill. Instill a habit of life-long learning, and your life will change forever.

Raise Your Standards

Whoever you are, whatever you've achieved, you can always be more. Do more. Take a hard look at your life. Is your career where you want it to be? How about your writing? If you're not happy with it, then it's time to raise your standards. Decide to change, to become a better, stronger version of you. It really is as simple as that. Your subconscious will help you grow, and if you put into practice the rest of the things in this book success is all but inevitable.

You'll also see this ripple across your entire life. If you raise your standards for writing, you'll become a successful author. Once you're a successful author you'll start looking at other areas of your life with an eye for improvement. I started with my body, and once I started to lose weight I focused on my career. Then my writing. I'm still making improvement today, but doing so is much, much easier than it used to be. I've gained momentum, and I've made success a habit.

Do the same. Your writing is the first hurdle, and right now it's as hard as it will ever be. If you start improving yourself today, then your standards *will* continue to rise. In a year you'll be achieving things everyone in your life thinks are impossible.

Become Positive

I spent a lot of my life as a realist, and an even larger part as a pessimist. If you'd told me five years ago I'd lose a hundred pounds, make a quarter of a million dollars a year, sell tens of thousands of books, become the lead software engineer at a cutting edge startup, or meet the girl of my dreams (mmm...Lisa), then I'd have told you that you were a fool.

Mindset. Is. Everything. The day I decided to become a more positive person my life began to change. Remember my little spiel about the power of belief? It's huge. If you believe in good things, then you will find them. Confucius said 'he who thinks he can and he who thinks he can't are both usually right'. Believe that you can accomplish things. Believe that good things will happen, and that the world can be a brighter place. Your quality of life will improve, and you'll be that much closer to accomplishing things most people believe are impossible.

Choosing to be positive and cheerful will have an immediate change on your daily life. You will be happier. You will rediscover enthusiasm. People will suddenly want to spend more time around you. Every part of your day will improve, all because your mindset is different. You can't control the events that occur, but you can absolutely control how you choose to interpret them.

Did someone just cut you off in traffic? Re-frame your usual reaction. You can get pissed off, or you can choose to assume that person didn't see you. Maybe their mother just died, and they're crying as they head to the funeral. You have no idea, so choose to believe the best. Anger hurts only you, so take a different path. You'll be glad you did.

Exercise #10- Pick one book and one podcast from the list above and subscribe to them. Now pick a time when you can listen to them each day. Commit to adding a new book every time you finish one.

Bonus: The next time something negative happens to you, practice re-framing it. What else could it mean? Maybe the lady at the grocery store didn't mean to steal your parking place. Maybe your boss's wife just left him. Remember, you can choose how you react to events.

11

READY, SET, HABIT

Okay, you have all the tools. You've learned all the pieces to a habit, you've learned the mindset, and you now possess a framework to set the right kind of goals. Now it's time to *build* the habit. As mentioned earlier, willpower doesn't last, but you're going to need it in the short term. The first three weeks of your new habit are critical, because your brain resists change until the habit is registered in your basal ganglia. If you haven't already started yours, we're going to make tomorrow day one.

Here's what you'll need to do to prepare:

Finger on the Trigger

As mentioned back in Chapter 2, a habit consists of three parts. The first part is the trigger. This is the event that causes your brain to execute the habit loop. It's time to pick your trigger, and it has to be consistent. This trigger should occur in the same time, and ideally the same place, every day. If you did the exercise in the Mornings Are Your Friend chapter, hopefully that time is in the early morning.

Once you have a time defined, you need to decide how you're going to trigger it. If it's early you can use an alarm. If it's later in the day you can use a reminder. If you can't define a specific time, then you need a circumstance to kick it off. The last is true for me. I get on the bus around 6:30 every morning. The instant I sit down I whip out my laptop and start writing. My trigger is the act of sitting down on the bus.

What's yours?

Build Your Routine

Now you need a routine, the body of the habit. Mine is opening the laptop, and selecting the document in Scrivener that I'm about to write in. I take a moment to read the chapter outline, then I start writing. Your routine may vary significantly from mine, and that's okay. It just has to be the same every day.

I highly recommend building a chain that takes you into writing. If you tap the alarm at six, then use the bathroom, then get oatmeal, then write, these events should occur in the same order every day. Your brain will begin to expect them, and within three weeks (probably less for most of you) your brain will be on autopilot. You'll wake up, tap the alarm, and the next conscious thought will be sitting down at your keyboard to write.

Engineer Your Reward

Once you finish your writing for the day, you need a suitable reward. This has to be something that you find stimulating. In my case, I finish by recording my word count, then I look at the image of my dream home I taped to the wall. I repeat to myself that I'm one day closer to being rich, and that I'm a better writer today than I was yesterday.

If that's too new-agey, feel free to buy yourself a latte. Whatever it takes so that your brain gets used to being rewarded for completing the habit.

Repurposing Habits

The assumption up to this point has been that you're creating your writing habit from scratch, but that may not be the case. You may already have a writing habit, and just need to tweak it to make it more consistent.

You might also have a habit that has nothing to do with writing, but that you can repurpose to fit writing. In either case I want you to think of your habit like the parts of an engine. The trigger, routine, and reward work together to form a complete functioning habit.

The beautiful thing is that you can swap out any one of the three parts and still maintain the habit. Instead of using three weeks of willpower to install a new one, why not change an existing habit?

This is accomplished by consciously examining the parts of the habit, then figuring out what part needs to change. For example, let's say you currently wake up to the alarm (trigger), get a cup of coffee and sit down at your computer to surf the web (routine), which relaxes you before you head off to work (reward).

You could repurpose this habit by replacing the routine, and you don't even have to change it all that much. Tomorrow you'd wake up to the alarm as usual, preserving the trigger. For your routine you'd still get your coffee, and still sit down at your computer. All you'd have to modify is adding a five minute writing sprint before you surf the web.

Your reward is the same. You're still relaxed for work, and were still able to browse Reddit, Facebook, or whatever sites you love. If you did this for a week, the five minute writing sprint would become a permanent part of the habit. You'd start doing it without thinking, which would pave the way to add longer sprints and less web surfing.

If you were previously surfing the web for thirty minutes you could eventually get to the point where you do a twenty-five minute sprint, and only spend the last five minutes surfing the web. Your brain would happily assume the habit hadn't changed, and would still give you the same feeling of relaxation you're enjoying. All this in spite of the fact that your routine has completely changed.

A Quick Note About Writing Sprints

Throughout the book you've heard me mention writing sprints, WPH (words per hour), and WPD (words per day). These concepts are fully explained in the first book in this series, *5,000 Words Per Hour.*

Lifelong Writing Habit is the get your butt in the chair book. 5KWPH is the book that will tell you how to be most efficient at writing once your butt is actually in that seat.

Exercise #11- It's time to engineer your writing habit. Take a good look at your daily routine. Where would the writing habit fit best? Can you re-purpose an existing habit, or do you need to create an entirely new one?

Either way, write out a promise to yourself about your new writing habit. Make it as specific as possible. It needs to include how and when you plan to write, how often, and what your reward will be.

Bonus: Set a reminder for one month from today. That reminder should ask you if you're still following through with your habit. Make that reminder repeat each and every month.

12

TROUBLESHOOTING

The number one reason people fail to write consistently is thinking in absolutes. If we mess up, then we inevitably beat ourselves up, giving in to the voice that says we can't do this. Impostor syndrome is a constant threat, one every writer wrestles with.

Here's the secret to beating it. You don't have to be James Joyce today. All you have to do is be a slightly better writer than you were yesterday. The knowledge that you have improved in some tiny way will be enough to sustain you until tomorrow, when you'll improve in another tiny way.

This process will continue for the rest of your life, which is where the title of this book comes from. Writing isn't a job. It isn't something you master, and it isn't something we choose to do for a paycheck.

Writing is a passion. It's an art, and it is a relentless taskmistress.

You need to understand that you're embarking on a lifelong journey, and right now you're near the beginning of that journey. You have thousands of miles to go, every one of them filled with wonder and discovery. Some days will require tedious hiking, but when you get to the top of a mountain and can see for miles it's all worth it.

You Will Screw Up

You're going to mess up. You'll miss days. You may occasionally fall off the wagon and stop writing entirely. I've done that more than once, in some cases for years. You know what? That's totally okay.

Writing is in your blood. If you make a mistake, don't beat yourself up about it. If you quit for a while, don't let that convince you that you're not a real writer. You are. Dust yourself off and get your ass back in that chair.

If you've finished a novel and it bombs, shake it off. If you write a draft and everyone hates it, shake it off. These are all stages on your journey. You need to be as relentless as the craft itself. Unreasonable goals require unreasonable expectations of yourself.

Also, remember that this isn't a solo journey. There are tens of thousands of writers in the trenches with you. Capitalize on that. Revisit the chapter on The Power of Your Peers if you need to. Find writers who can help lift you back up, and who you can lift up in turn.

They'll tell you what part of you already knows. Making mistakes is not only okay, it's impossible to avoid. The question is, will you learn from them, or let them make you quit?

Dealing With Excuses

This book looks great on paper, right? You just decide to write, and WHAM you're a writer cranking out book after book. But what if that doesn't happens? What if you wake up tomorrow and you just can't make yourself get in the chair and write?

Many people reading this have read a ton of books on self-improvement. Most of us have tried this stuff before, but sometimes we just can't make ourselves do the work we need to do. We'll rational-ize. We're tired. We've been working hard at our day jobs, or as parents. We're stressed. We'll do it tomorrow. It's okay to take one day off, right?

Fuck that. You don't get to take a day off. You don't get to wait until tomorrow. You need to write today, and every day that follows. It needs to become something you do every day without thinking, and you'd no more skip it than skip brushing your teeth or eating breakfast.

If you aren't able to make yourself do that, then quite simply your reasons aren't strong enough. That target identity isn't compelling enough. The life you want isn't real enough in your mind. More likely, the pain isn't great enough.

Nothing is as dangerous to you as mediocrity. If you're looking at your writing life right now and saying it's good enough, then you'll never find the drive to improve it. You need to be appalled by what you see, and you need to raise your standards to match the person you want to become.

If you run into this, I want you to ask yourself this question. When you are on your deathbed looking back, how will Future You feel about the fact that you took today off? Today led to taking tomorrow off, which led to taking next month off. You never finished all the books you could have written, never left the legacy you were meant to, all because you didn't write today.

Your daily writing is *that* important, and Future You is watching. Don't disappoint them. You know you are capable of more, so get your ass in that chair and do the work. Every day. You know you're capable of it, and Future You is already thanking you from your mansion on the beach.

Long Term Thinking

Like I said above, writing is a lifelong journey, but it's easy for us to get caught in the little things. This is especially true if you're writing your first novel. I remember that well, and at that stage your novel is your baby. The book is everything. It's not only your finest work, it's your only work.

When you're a little further along in your career and you have six or seven books under your belt, your perspective changes. You remember the first book fondly, but it doesn't have the same impact that it once did. Bad reviews won't shake you, because you've seen them before.

Everything gets easier with time and experience. So if you're at the stage where you only have one or two books out please take this to heart: It will get better, and it will become easier. All you have to do is keep writing, and keep learning.

Lifelong Habit

I'd like to offer a final caveat. I chose the title of this book for many reasons. One of the most important is the neurological significance of habits. They live in your brain forever. Once you've created a habit it never goes away. Ever.

This is the reason why alcoholics have to be so careful about drinking. Their destructive habits lurk at the edges of their consciousness, waiting to re-assert themselves. People who've lost a lot of weight sometimes regain it all plus some, for the same reason.

Here's the good news. If you can build a writing habit, you'll have it for life. Even if you fall off the wagon and stop writing for a few months the habit still exists. All you have to do is use it again, and your brain will happily strengthen it and allow it back into your daily routine.

So don't beat yourself up if you fall off the wagon. Just get your ass back in that chair and start writing. You're going to accomplish great things, because *you are a lifelong writer.*

Exercise #12- Set a one month, three month, six month, and twelve month reminder for yourself. Mine says 'Are you still writing?'

The purpose of these reminders is simple. If you fall off the wagon and stop writing, they'll nudge you. If you get one of them and realize you're not writing, don't beat yourself up. Just sit down and start writing.

Bonus: Pick out your next writing book right now, and go buy it. Once you've finished the exercises in this one, start reading the next one. If you haven't picked up 5,000 Words Per Hour, it is a great next step.

I have a ton of craft books listed over at www.chrisfoxwrites.com. Just go to the For Writers page, and you'll have enough other books to get you through the next year.

WHERE TO GO FROM HERE

Congratulations, my friend, you've completed this book. I know it's not terribly long, but we covered a lot of information. There are a whole bunch of exercises, and you may not have done any of them. If you're like me you may have read straight through and said you'll do them later.

If that's the case I urge you to continue to the next page where I've compiled all the exercises. Do the work. This book will be useless to you unless you sit down at the keyboard and actually crank out words.

Start your writing habit TODAY. Track the results. You WILL improve, and in a month you'll be much faster than you are now. In three months, you'll look back at today as the day that changed your writing life forever.

Or set this book aside and start looking for other books, podcasts, or videos about writing. If you do, you can read all about success, but you'll never achieve it. That takes work. A lot of work. Work I'm hoping you're willing to commit to, because if you are you will amaze yourself.

I hope you've found this book helpful. If you have, I encourage you to sign up to the mailing list to be notified when the next Write Faster, Write Smarter book is released. I'd also be grateful if you'd consider leaving a review wherever you bought it. As most of you know, they're critically important to the success of any author's books.

Either way, I'd like to thank you for sharing your time with me. I'd love to hear from you, so feel free to contact me at chris@chrisfoxwrites.com to tell me how the program is working out for you, to make suggestions, or just to connect.

If you're interested, I've created a Facebook group for authors to meet and discuss their progress. Just shoot me an email, and I'm happy to add you!

Sincerely,
Chris Fox

EXERCISES

Exercise #1- Write out your daily routine as a list of habits. Next to each of those habits put a (G) or a (B) for good or bad. Once you've completed the list pick a habit you'd like to flip. We're going to modify that habit in future chapters, until it becomes the foundation of your daily writing. For now all you have to do is pick it!

Exercise #2- Write a paragraph about your target identity. Hell, write three paragraphs. Make it as vivid as possible. Describe your perfect writing life, the kind you'd have if you tirelessly cranked out 5,000 words a day for the next three years.

Then write out your purpose. Why are you doing all this work?

Finally answer the two big questions. Is this achievable? Is it worth it?

Now print out a copy and put it up wherever you write. Look at it every day when you sit down to write.

Bonus: Find a picture of the house you want to own, or the beach you want to write on, or something that represents the life you're going to have when you become your target identity. Put it up next to the written description.

Exercise #3- Decide how you are going to track your writing habit. Maybe you need a physical calendar, where you jot the words down on the date each time you write. Maybe you use a spreadsheet. Maybe you download the 5000 Words Per Hour app I wrote to track writing sprints (if you have an iPhone or iPad).

The method you choose is completely up to you, but the critical factor here is that you MUST track your daily writing. You must log the date, and the number of words you wrote. I know that sounds small, but this will have a POWERFUL effect on your writing.

Exercise #4- Search your hard drive, email, or file cabinet for the oldest piece of your writing you can find. Go back and read it with a critical eye. What have you learned since then? How has your writing improved? Look at all the progress you've made since then. Imagine how much better you'll be in a year if you practice daily.

Exercise #5- This one is a biggie. Develop your system. Either choose an app, or create a pen and paper system where you can track your writing projects. Then write down every project you can think of until every last one is out of your head and in the system.

Bonus 1- Clear your inbox using the methodology

above. Practice keeping it clean for a week. The
results will probably surprise you.

Bonus 2- Put *all* your projects into your system, not
just the writing ones. This will have a massive
impact on your overall productivity and happiness,
plus you'll be more attractive.

Exercise #6- Make a list of your biggest distractions,
the things that most often prevent you from writing.
Maybe that's binge-watching Scrubs on Netflix.
Maybe it's being constantly interrupted by loved
ones in need of help. Whatever they are, see if you
can brainstorm some ways to erect barriers around
the things that are preventing you from writing.

Bonus: Do the same thing for the good behaviors.
Make a list of things that will simplify your writing,
so that all you have to do is sit down at your
computer and GO.

Exercise #7- Set your alarm 15 minutes earlier than normal. Before you go to bed have your computer primed and ready. Use propinquity to make sure all you have to do is sit down and write. When you wake up write for 10 minutes. See how it feels. You probably won't be very fast at first, but that's okay. If you repeat this every day you'll improve rapidly. If you like the process you can increase the time you write.

Bonus: Download my 5,000 Words Per Hour App, or use a timer to conduct a writing sprint. If you aren't familiar with the process, feel free to check out *5,000 Words Per Hour* the book, which explains how writing sprints work and how you can maximize your writing time. Reading 5KWPH isn't necessary to developing a writing habit, but it will make you far more productive, which is especially handy for those of us with busy lives.

Exercise #8- Write out your short term goals for your daily habit. When will you start? How long will you write? How many words are you aiming for each day? Be as specific as possible. Then write out your long term goals, ideally for the next 12 months. Where do you want to be in a year? How many books will you write? How long will each take using your short term goals?

Bonus: Create reminders both for your short term and long term goals. Your calendar or smartphone should notify you when a goal comes due. Each day it will ping you to let you know you should be writing, and it should also notify you when it expects a project to be completed (I'll have *Vampires Don't Sparkle* re-written and submitted to Tammi by September 28th. Bam, I get a reminder on September 28th checking to make sure I did that).

Exercise #9- Write down the top five supporters in your life. These are the people who empower and support you, and also the people you should be spending more time with. If you don't have five, or don't have any, that's okay. Now write down the top five negative people in your life. These are the people who are always complaining, the people who tell you that 'it can't be done'. Almost all of us have at least one, so write down up to five.

Now take a hard look at both lists. Brainstorm ways to spend more time with the positive column. If the positive column is empty, I want you to email me at chris@chrisfoxwrites.com. I'd be proud to be the first person you add to that column, and I'm happy to connect you with like-minded people.

On the negative list, you need to make a decision about each person. Is this someone you should be associating with? Or are they the type of psychic vampire who will suck away your positive energy? If they're the latter, is there any reason to keep them in your life? If you have to (in the case of family), how can you minimize the impact they have on your daily life?

Bonus: Email your favorite author and ask them to be your mentor.

∾

Exercise #10- Pick one book and one podcast from the list above and subscribe to them. Now pick a time when you can listen to them each day.

Commit to adding a new book every time you finish one.

Bonus: The next time something negative happens to you, practice re-framing it. What else could it mean? Maybe the lady at the grocery store didn't mean to steal your parking place. Maybe your boss's wife just left him. Remember, you can choose how you react to events.

Exercise #11- It's time to engineer your writing habit. Take a good look at your daily routine. Where would the writing habit fit best? Can you re-purpose an existing habit, or do you need to create an entirely new one?

Either way, write out a promise to yourself about your new writing habit. Make it as specific as possible. It needs to include how and when you plan to write, how often, and what your reward will be.

Bonus: Set a reminder for one month from today. That reminder should ask you if you're still following through with your habit. Make that reminder repeat each and every month.

Exercise #12- Set a one month, three month, six month, and twelve month reminder for yourself. Mine says 'Are you still writing?'

The purpose of these reminders is simple. If you fall off the wagon and stop writing, they'll nudge you. If you get one of them and realize you're not writing, don't beat yourself up. Just sit down and start writing.

Bonus: Pick out your next writing book right now, and go buy it. Once you've finished the exercises in this one, start reading the next one. If you haven't picked up 5,000 Words Per Hour, it is a great next step.

I have a ton of craft books listed over at www.chrisfoxwrites.com. Just go to the For Writers page, and you'll have enough other books to get you through the next year.

ABOUT THE AUTHOR

By day I am an iPhone developer architecting the app used to scope Stephen Colbert's ear. By night I am Batman. Okay maybe not. One can dream though, right?

I've been writing since I was six years old, and started inflicting my work on others at age 18. By age 24 people stopped running away when I approached them with a new story and shortly thereafter I published my first one in *The Rifter*.

Wait, you're still reading?

Ok, the facts I'm supposed to list in a bio. As of this writing I'm 38 years old and live just north of the Golden Gate Bridge in the beautiful town of Mill Valley. If you're unsure how to find it just follow the smell of self-entitlement. Once you see the teens driving Teslas you'll know you're in the right place.

I live in a tiny studio that I can cross in (literally)

five steps, and don't own an oven. But you know what? It's worth it. I love developing iPhone apps and if you want to work in San Francisco you accept that the rent for a tiny place costs more than most people's mortgage.

If you and about 2 million other people start buying my books I promise to move out of Marin to a house in the redwoods up in Guerneville. No pressure. Wait, that's a lie. Pressure.

For more information:

www.chrisfoxwrites.com

Made in the USA
Middletown, DE
10 September 2019